This Tedious Journey

JOURNALING YOUR CHRISTIAN WALK

Nastassia A. Muhammad

This Tedious Journey
journaling your Christian walk....

Copyright © 2019 by Nastassia Muhammad/I.C.P
All rights reserved solely by the author. The author guarantees all contents are original and do not infringe upon the legal rights of any other person or work. No part of this book may be reproduced in any form without the permission of the author. The views expressed in this book are not necessarily those of the publisher.

ISBN 978-1-7321084-1-7

Unless otherwise indicated, Bible quotations are taken from the King James Version. Copyright 2000 by Oxford University Press, USA.

Edited by
Marilyn Fenderson Ministries

Published by
Insightful Creation Publication
www.insightfulcp.com

Printed in the United States of America
First Printing, 2019

Acknowledgements

First and foremost, all praises be to my Heavenly Father. Thank you Lord for your vision for my life. Thank you for taking this journey with me. I wouldn't have done it without. As I continue to this journey, I will always remember my purpose and how important it is to tell my testimony.

Thank you to my Mom (Pastor Marilyn Fenderson) my editor, constant supporter and my number one fan. Thank you for assisting me through my journey and this creative process. For always being there when I needed you the most and helping to bring my vision to life.

To my Dad (Francis Fenderson), Brother (Trey Fenderson), and best friend (Kishonda) for your constant support. For the words said that changed my life, and for constantly uplifting me when this journey became too hard to bare.

Thank you to Spirit and Life Coach, (Shakesha Dye) in whom this journey was originally inspired by. Journeying alone can be troublesome. Thank you for being the beacon of light, the instrument of God and for challenging my thinking and helping me get to my authentic self.

Thanks to so many others who understood my vision and supported it. A special thanks to those who gave me a chance to share my testimony. Monichia Beal, Shekila Reed and family, just to name a few.

Table of Contents

Foreword 9

Preface 11

Let's Define Wisdom, Shall We 13

The Belly of the Whale 25

This Tedious Journey Begins 33

Mirror, Mirror 39

Ease on Down the Road 47

Got to Give It Up 57

Don't Push Me, I'm Close To the Edge 65

I see the Light 83

Faith without Works 93

How Tedious was your journey? 105

Foreword

By: Pastor Marilyn Fenderson

The Author, Nastassia A Muhammad, does an excellent job of outlining her Christian walk. Although the journey may have been tedious, it was all in God's plan to get her to a position of peace and purpose.

Her book "This Tedious Journey" is a perfect example of God at work. Through her journey, He revealed a gift that she didn't realize she had, the gift to write. I love how she provides a way for the reader to connect with her story. This approach provides a means of interaction which enables you to journal your life's experiences as it relates to hers.

As Humans, we all have a journey which dictates our story as well as the path that leads to the plan that God has for our lives. This journey defines our spiritual growth and ultimately reveals our purpose and God given gifts. Our testimonies are not only cathartic for us, but they serve as healing and restoration for others.

Oftentimes, our journey is one that we must travel regardless of how tedious or difficult. However, as we journey through life, there are some things that we must go through. God sees what needs to be developed in us, so He takes us through a refinement process by testing us in the areas that need change.

Some of us may lack patience, so he will place us in a situation where we learn to wait. Some may lack peace, so he will place you in a situation where you learn how to be still. That just shows how much he loves you, he will develop in you the fruits that are needed to navigate through life.

I am fully persuaded that God's promises will be manifested in your lives as she walks you through her journey. So, sit back and enjoy the experience!

Preface

This book is the result of telling God "yes" to his will. Had it been up to me, I would have never done this. I laid in my bed one Sunday morning, skipping church obviously, to spend time with God. While basking in His glory, He said so loud and clear, "Write the book".

As I begin to submit my life to Christ wholeheartedly, I faced some challenges that were seldomly spoken about in church. Therefore, I had a hard time knocking down the obstacles that blocked my growth. Sometimes I would over complicate my thinking which caused a lack of understanding of what was happening to me. I'm pretty sure I'm not the only one who has asked a lot of questions and received little answers.

This book explains the answers that I received through an incredible source, who helped to guide me through all my feelings and emotions. Through transparency, I have revealed my thoughts behind certain events that took place as well as some of the things that I struggled with.

Some of the views that I have expressed in this book are based on my perspective, and not necessarily fact.

Chapter One
Let's Define Wisdom, Shall We

Wisdom can be attained no matter what age you are. Sometimes people don't realize how much crap you've gone through in your lifetime? It's enough to make anyone irrational, let alone dysfunctional. So, don't allow people to discredit what you've gone through, they don't know your story.

I'll bet it makes you feel like you didn't earn your wisdom, right? And who says that wisdom only belongs to the "old folks"? Now don't get me wrong, it is their wisdom that has probably kept you from doing half of the stupid things that you've done in your life. Nevertheless, the only reason they have so much wisdom is because of their life's journey.

Believe it or not, that's how wisdom is developed. It's the knowledge and understanding that you gain from life's experiences.

Those experiences are then transformed to lessons learned. <u>So, I want you to ponder this; would you go back and repeat the same stupid mistakes after you have learned valuable lessons,</u> I didn't think so.

Years from now you will be able to tell some young soul about the things you have learned. Just like the "old folk" did with you. How ironic, the same group of individuals that we talk about are the same ones that we become.

You see, we are all a part of a certain developmental lifecycle. Everyone who exist, no matter what color, race, creed, background or age, have a distinct role that contributes to how we navigate in this world. We are a community of believers; no man is an island and without each other we wouldn't be able to experience the diverse qualities that makes us who we are.

> *(Corinthians 12:12 KJV) "For as the body is one, and hath many members, and all the members of that one body, being many, are one body: so also is Christ."*

I said all that to say this, wisdom is not given to just our elders, it is given to anyone who is able and willing to pay attention and learn life's lessons. You see, life is a school and class is now in session. Are you going to be the one that passes the course, or the one who flunks it just to start all over again to try and learn the same lessons?

We could all stand to learn a thing or two, even when we think we have it all figured out. So, no matter what you go through or what you've been through, open yourself up to receive more wisdom. I guarantee it will make life a very interesting school to attend.

Time to Reflect. *Use this time to think about some of the mistakes that have been made in your life. What would you have done differently? Would you go back and change how you handled things? What was the valuable lesson learned? Use this time to be extremely honest with yourself. Nobody knows you like you know you. And this is a safe space for you to go ahead and unload my love.*

During my Christian walk, I always hear about how the saints prevail through trials and tribulations, the victorious parts of their testimony is always told. However, I think people sometimes skip the details, thus leaving out the true sentiments of their journey with Christ.

In my observations, I found that people tend to feel embarrassed when they talk about the hard times of serving Christ. Religion often confounds us to only see the upside. If we are not careful, we will think that God only wants us to be faultless and that He will only reward our perfections. What we don't realize is that God doesn't expect for us to be perfect.

Since the beginning of creation, God had to rebuke mankind and reteach lessons time and time again until we pass the test. God knows who we are, but the more you get to know Him, the more He changes you. You see, He knows that we are all imperfect people and that's what makes us perfect to be used for His glory.

I have parents who have a great relationship with God and they've always stressed that true worship comes from your relationship with Him. Religion was overrated in our household, so I was raised to have a healthy balance of living my life and walking with God. But somehow, I got into the mindset that God would only love me if I did things right.

Coming up, I attended a few churches that seemed to condemn you if you weren't conforming to their idea of holiness. You could only listen to gospel music, you couldn't wear pants or makeup, or you could only have Godly thoughts. They didn't teach me how to be in the world and not of the world. I later learned that holiness is not a dress style, it is a lifestyle and a mind reset. As long as I am in the perfect will of God, I am acceptable in His sight.

> ***(Romans 12:2 KJV) "And be not conformed to this world: but be ye transformed by the renewing of your mind, that ye may prove what is that good, and acceptable, and perfect will of God."***

I always knew that I was set apart, but there was always the struggle of trying to belong or trying to find my place. As a young girl growing up in this society, I was very impressionable, so fitting in seemed like the right thing to do. My mom would tell me to develop a close relationship with God and experience him for myself but that didn't sync in until I got good and grown.

So now here I am, living my life and just learning to balance. Truth be told, I put a lot of pressure on myself. I thought I had to be perfect all the time.

Not only did I feel that God had certain expectations of me, I also had certain expectations of myself. I was harder on me than anyone else could be. When I look at my family, they've accomplished so much, so I felt that I had to measure up somehow, some way. Not understanding that the strain I put on myself drove me away from God.

Here He is trying to make me understand that I'm already awesome in his sight, but I was fighting my own learning process. So, in essence, I was telling God that what He was doing in me, was not good enough and that I was in charge of me.

Let me tell you, it took me a long time and I mean a long time to accept what God was doing with me. I fought tooth and nail over this journey, I was so stuck in the old me and afraid to let go of the things that I felt protected me. My sanity and my refuge were at stake, so I was very reluctant to discard everything that was comfortable, and everything that I knew to embark on this unfamiliar territory.

Time to Reflect: *So, tell me my Love, what are you afraid to let go of? What is keeping you from being your best self? Is there any pain that holds you back from being free? What made you build up your walls to protect yourself?*

Chapter Two
The Belly of the Whale

There is a story in the bible that talks about a man named Jonah. Jonah was a prophet of God who was given instructions to deliver a message to a certain group of people that dwelt in Nineveh. However, Jonah had other plans, he didn't want to deliver the message to the people because of his hatred for them, so he disobeyed God and went to another city.

Because of his disobedience, God allowed him to get swallowed by a whale. He was in the belly of that whale for three days, but during those days Jonah prayed and cried out to God. Only then was he able to examine himself and realize that he was no different than the people that God had call him to preach to.

> *(Jonah 2:1, 2 KJV) "Then Jonah prayed unto the Lord his God out of the fish's belly, And said, I cried by reason of mine affliction unto the Lord and he heard me; out of the belly of hell cried I, and thou heardest my voice."*

It was about two years ago when I started my journey. I can remember the day I gave God my full attention. I had just gotten out of an imbalanced relationship. This individual sucked me dry, the crazy part was that I allowed it. I let him drain me of my emotion, my spirituality, my purpose, my finances and my very reason for being. Sounds drastic, right?

At the time, I didn't realize it because when we broke up, I became really angry with God. I was trying to figure out why he would put me in this situation to fail, because I felt like I had done all I could to make it work. After all, I hadn't been in a relationship in a very long time and when I finally do it ends up like this.

I went to the park near my house and sat on the bench and just cried out to God. Not really knowing what to say, or how to speak. Hurting so much that I couldn't even pray about it. At first, I tried to carry on as if it didn't bother me, not really vocalizing how much I was hurting. That day at the park, sitting on that bench, I was angry, frustrated, lost, and not even knowing where to go from that point. That Jonah in the belly of the whale experience was real. If I never understood that story before, I understood it at that moment.

So, I sat there, very confused and angry at the same time. Suddenly, I got a phone call from one of my spiritual leaders. I would like to believe that God was sitting there shaking His head saying, "let me send this foolish girl some help."

God had talked to her about me, little ole' me. It was at that moment that the process began. I had been emptied of everything just so I could be filled with the right things this time. Lo and behold my journey begins.

You see, God wants the very best for us. He wants us to have a strong foundation so that we can prosper in society and not be unstable because of what the world shows us. God talks about us being the clay, and He is the potter. He makes us, breaks us, and makes us again.

> *(Jeremiah 18:6 KJV) "O house of Israel, cannot I do with you as this potter? Saith the Lord. Behold, as the clay is in the potter's hand, so are ye in mine hand, O house of Israel."*

We as human beings are flawed, and God is fully aware of that. But in order to possess the characteristics of Christ, He puts us in situations that bring out the qualities that He wants us to have. I would like to think of that moment in the park as God having a huge smirk on His face, rubbing His hands together and saying, "Now it's time."

I've been saved since I was nine years old, having had some great experiences with God but I was hiding. I didn't really care to be in the forefront, but wouldn't you know it, that is exactly where God would always push me to be.

Nevertheless, I didn't want to risk failure, so it was easier to shrink into the background. After all, I've failed many times before and the thought of experiencing more failures was just something I didn't want to do anymore.

What's crazy is that there were moments in my life that when I was put in the forefront, I was truly amazing. However, that was not a comfortable place for me, so back to hiding I went, it was so much safer there.

So here I go, having no clue what this journey entailed, I just know that it was going to be a lot of hard work. But I was ready to do something different. They say the definition of insanity is doing the same thing and expecting different results. I was sick of the ordinary, I was over being mediocre and I was ready to embark upon this new journey in hopes to gain so much more than what I've allowed myself to become accustomed to.

Time to Reflect: *So, let's dig in my Love! At what point did you discover that you were\are in a really bad place? What are some habits or characteristics that you discovered you have\had? Did you actually take the time to uncover these things about you? If not, are you at least aware of these things about you?*

Chapter Three
This Tedious Journey Begins

So, where do I start? All I can remember is feeling that I knew enough about God and how He operates, but boy was I wrong. I had to gain some great insight on how I perceived my God. To think I had put Him in a neat little box my whole Christian walk, never really tapping into the true nature of who He is, let alone understanding my identity in Him.

So, I had to go back to the basics, it was like teaching an adult how to do addition. Really!!! I know who I am, at least that's what I told myself but then I had to dig a little deeper. Do I really understand who I am? Because truth be told, since I was a child, I let others define who I was. They told me I was fat, they told me I was sensitive, they told me I was defensive, argumentative and so many other things.

As I grew older, I started to believe those things, so much so that I didn't want to reveal myself for fear of those labels and for fear that those things about me where true. And if you know me, I'm determined to prove people wrong. I'm not what you think I am, nor what you say I am.

So, who am I in God? Well he calls me, a chosen generation, a royal priesthood, a holy generation, a peculiar people.

(1 Peter 2:9 KJV) "But ye are a chosen generation, a royal priesthood, an holy nation, a peculiar people; that ye should shew forth the praises of him who hath called you out of darkness into his marvelous light."

My sole intention is to have dominion and authority over this world and the things in it. What's crazy is that once life happens, we tend to forget all that stuff. It's easy to claim to be God's child but it requires a steadfast mind to walk in it. So, I had to tear down every wall that I had built to protect myself and take on a totally different mindset. Let me tell you, that's the part that hurts. Think about this, if you have a tattoo, you endured a lot of pain because ink is literally being imbedded in your skin. The finished product is beautiful, but the process is unpleasant.

However, it hurts even worse when you get the tattoo removed, because it requires you to experience the pain all over again. That's how it feels when undoing the damaged that you've done to yourself, you must relive the pain in order to get to your healing, go figure. It was in that pain that this tedious journey was birthed.

I was afraid of the unknown, so the thought of losing control of my own path towards my destiny was crazy to me. Nonetheless, I had to remember that God called me out of the darkness into His marvelous light and I am finally seeing the light.

I know I'm not the only one. How many times have you flipped out because things weren't in your control? Or at least felt some kind of way about it. Let's face it, we all want our way in some shape, form, or fashion, some of us just hate to admit it...like me, LOL

Time to Reflect: *So, tell me my Love, how do you feel when you are not in control? At what point in your life did you discover that you had to take control of your life? What life event occurred that made you feel helpless?*

Chapter Four
Mirror, Mirror

"I'm starting with the man in the mirror, I'm asking him to change his ways. And no message could have been any clearer, if you want to make the world a better place take a look at yourself and make a change."

These lyrics written by Siedah Garret and Glen Ballard, bare some of the most insightful words that I've ever heard spoken from an artist. It is necessary that change starts from within. However, exploring the depths of myself was painful.

I am somewhat of a perfectionist, which might not sound so bad, but I hate to fail. I hate the idea of losing, in any way, shape or form and when I feel like I've lost I don't respond well. Talk about some truth, that's a pill I had to swallow.

My Spirit and life coach said that I was spoiled, and I always like pretty images, LOL. Meaning, I don't like for bad things to happen. I pretty much like for things to be fairytale like, I had to swallow that pill too. This was just some of the few things that I learned about myself and had to come to terms with.

It's so funny how God works, I mentioned earlier that when you ask for something, God puts you in situations to help you apply what you ask for. I think Morgan Freeman said it best in the movie *Evan Almighty,* and I'll paraphrase, "When you ask God for courage, he doesn't just magically give you courage, but He puts you in situations to help you exercise courage."

Man was He right, I asked God to expand my territory, and to increase me. Well little did I know, this required me to establish a stronger spiritual foundation. So, I had to dig deeper when I discovered these things about myself.

I had to get to know Jesus personally, as if I didn't know Him already or did I really know him? So, the first question is, how did I see Him before? Well, he was the End All Be All, El Numero Uno, Almighty God, Everlasting Father, and much more.

Now did I treat Him like that? No, I treated Him like a dictator, a punisher for when I did wrong. As a result, I hid from Him when I did things wrong, like a dog hiding from its owner when it does something bad. I felt like God would repay me for my wrong, and as long as I was doing well, I would be ok. I expected for God to be hard on me like I was on myself.

In certain religious and/or spiritual backgrounds, some teach the disciplined concept, which is the very foundation of spirituality. Oftentimes, there is a certain standard that you are expected to live up to. However, there is more to it than just that, God's intended purpose for us was to establish relationship.

> *(Matthew 22:37 KJV) "Jesus said unto him, Thou shalt love the Lord thy God with all thy heart and with all thy soul and with all thy mind."*

Since the very beginning Adam and Eve were created to glorify the love and relationship of God. The Garden of Eden was considered that special place where Adam and God could commune, so relationship is very important.

Like a father to a child, Dad desires to have a relationship with us. Although Dad might not like some of the things that we do, he would never disown us. He may chastise us because that's what good fathers do but He would never want to see us fail. We must be able to learn from the mistakes that we make. Otherwise, we would never be functional adults in an ever-changing world.

This alone changed my mind about God. To know that He longs for me just as I should long for Him has set me free.

I began to think about my relationships with my earthly fathers. I had two fathers, both biological and step-father. The two of them equally contributed to teaching me many lessons in life.

Most of all, they set the standard for how I should be treated when a man comes in my life. So now there are certain expectations that I've set for myself.

When I think about it, one cherished and spoiled me while the other chastised and disciplined me. What a perfect balance, this was the ultimate example of how God loved me. He shows us compassion, but He also disciplines us to keep us from going down the wrong path. What parent would want to see their child in harm's way? I don't know of any.

> *(Hebrews 12:7 KJV) "If ye endure chastening, God dealeth with you as with sons, for what son is he whom the father chasteneth not?"*

I was extremely grateful when I thought about this. I realized that my relationship with God had already been established and He used the relationship of my fathers to demonstrate how much He cared for me.

Time to Reflect: *Can you be honest with me? When you look in the mirror, what do you see? Do you love or hate what you see? If there was something about you that could change, what would it be? What do you think God thinks about you? Do you think He would be disappointed in what He sees?*

Chapter Five
Ease on Down the Road

If you've ever seen *"The Wiz"* you will understand exactly what I mean by *"Ease on Down the Road"*. This phrase comes from the song written by *Charlie Smalls* which resonates in my heart.

In a particular scene, Dorothy and her friends embarked on a journey in search of the yellow brick road to find certain attributes that they lacked. The song encourages them to see the yellow brick road as direction towards self-discovery and purpose. They later discovered that the very thing they were searching for, they possessed the whole time.

"Don't you carry nothing that might be a load, come on ease on down, ease on down the road." How interesting, we are instructed to unload the burdens that keep us down and to cast our cares on God. But, just like human nature, we tend to take all our baggage everywhere we go.

In discovering myself, I was a self-proclaimed bag lady and I tried to convince God that my baggage was necessary in my growth. Only for Him to tell me that I had to let these things go. Let it go? How can I let all the hurts, failures, pains and traumatic experiences go?

As I begin to reflect on these things, God brought to mind that my experiences are what allowed me to build barriers. These barriers were keeping me from experiencing God to the fullest. I was weighted down, tired, angry and frustrated of the things that happened in my past.

I was extremely hard on myself and would never admit defeat. I was my own worst enemy and had put so much pressure on myself. I thought that I wasn't worthy of God's love because of the mistakes that I've made. Often wondering if I was devoid of purpose and unfit to be used by God.

The same way I thought God to be in my life was the same way I thought of myself. Since I perceived God to be the punisher, I was that to myself. Not forgiving myself of the failures and the mistakes, I placed all those burdens on myself instead of turning them over to God. I later discovered that my burdens were too heavy for me to carry, that's why God tells us to lay down every weight and the sin that so easily beset us.

> *(Hebrews 12:1 KJV) "Wherefore seeing we also are compassed about with so great a cloud of witnesses, let us lay aside every weight, and the sin which doth so easily beset us, and let us run with patience the race that is set before us."*

Our burdens slow us down from the progression of life. Not only that, they keep us from experiencing the true nature of God. You see, God represents freedom. The scripture says, where the spirit of the Lord is, there is liberty.

> **(2 Cor. 3:17 KJV) "Now the Lord is that Spirit and where the spirit of the Lord is here is liberty."**

So, I had to liberate myself of the past and realize that the things that have happened in my life, whether good or bad, happened to teach me something. Understanding not to focus on the event itself, but to focus on the lesson that comes from experiencing the event.

However, when you are overzealous in your own thoughts and hyperactive in your thinking, like me, it's kind of hard not to think about the event. That's where I struggled the most.

I also had to learn to forgive myself because I had held myself in condemnation. Meaning I blamed myself for every imperfect thing that I had done. It's enough for others to be against you, but when you are against yourself that's a serious problem. I had to realize that as much as I wanted to be perfect and as much as I strived to be perfect, I am only human.

God has always given me an eloquence for words and there were points in my life when God used me to inspire others. I wanted it to stay that way, to know that I was someone's rock. Not thinking that I needed a rock for myself because trying to live up to other people's expectations was exhausting. I wanted to be the end all be all, until I got tired.

I'm sure you understand how that feels, trying to be there for so many people. Being the one that holds others down, but then you look around and not too many people are holding you down. My advice to you is free yourself, people's expectations will rob you of your freedom. It's like someone putting you in a bubble and expecting you to perform in that bubble. I had to respect myself to know that I deserve liberation and that it is okay to put myself first.

Although I might not be perfect, my flaws are all a part of God's plan. After all, we are all works in progress, so we strive to be perfect, but we fall short daily. God knows that humans are flawed, He is the only perfect being. We are imperfect people, living in an imperfect world, yet we serve a perfect God.

Why do you think God sent prophets to deliver messages of destruction when man began to operate in sin and disobedience? He knew man was flawed and did not possess the faith to understand who He was nor the trust to know that He loved them.

We as humans oftentimes can't see what's already in front of us. We have a tendency to want to see things before we accept them as truth. Therefore, God had to send his Son Jesus Christ in the form of man to give us something tangible to believe in. It is through His death and resurrection that we are free.

After Jesus was sacrificed, we could throw away the pressure of being perfect. Now I'm not saying that because we are under grace and mercy that we can now just do whatever we want. God still holds us accountable for our actions, however we are free to make mistakes and learn from them. That is the beauty of being in relationship with God, He allows me room to grow and change.

It's the times when we are in our worst moments that He touches us and teaches us, molds us and shapes us, then builds and perfects us to be used for His glory. I'm sure you've heard the saying "God doesn't call the qualified, He qualifies the called."

Can you honestly say that if you hadn't made the mistakes you made that you would be where you are now? Sound familiar? I now know that He is using me as an example of His goodness and mercy to demonstrate to others that He loves us even with our flaws.

Time to Reflect: *Here is a chance to unload. What are you holding yourself accountable for? Is this accountability helping you or destroying you? What do you need to free yourself of? Who do you need to free yourself from?*

Chapter Six
Got to Give It Up

Did I mention that this journey was not easy? All the revelation that I received was what I needed, but guess what? I had to pay a price. God called me into seclusion and there was only a select few that were allowed to teach, inspire, and aid in my transfiguration. My family of course and a select group of friends were the only ones I had to rely on in my quiet season.

Around the beginning stages of my journey, I had to leave my comfort zone and embark on unfamiliar territory. I picked up and moved from my hometown Chicago, where I was born and raised, to Atlanta, GA. What a change of mindset and a real culture shock. Atlanta isn't bad, but it definitely isn't Chicago, so I had to adjust to the change.

Here I am away from my family and my stability, but God said I had to give all of that up for my growth. As much as my family loves me and I love them, God had to isolate me in order to strengthen my Christian walk. The ole' saints use to say, get to know God for yourself and in that moment, I had to.

The people who I thought were supposed to be close friends, I ended up losing. So, during my transition, I had no one in Atlanta to really turn to that I could trust. There was one friend in particular that encouraged me to move there but when I finally did, there were some unforeseen circumstances which prevented us from remaining friends. As bad as the situation was, I knew God was calling me to a great deal of isolation.

There were moments when I was upset that it had to be this individual because I adored this person deeply and I still do but I had to look at the greater picture. The direction that I was headed, only a few were able to help aid me in my journey. So, God used this person to teach me a lesson, a lesson that hurt no doubt because it was hard for me to lose true friends, nonetheless it was a lesson that I had to learn. There were a few others that I had to loosen myself from, people who meant the world to me, but I saw those relationships fade away as well.

When you are serious about where God wants to take you, you must be strong enough and be ready to give up the things and people you love. There are some individuals in your life that can't aid in your growth and it's nothing against them, but you must be protected from them.

If, and only if God is the head of your life, then you must let Him order your steps. He can see things coming before we can and we have to be willing to accept what is and what should be, even when it hurts us the most.

There were some behaviors I had to change as well, and sex was one of them. First and foremost, let me just say that I thought I would never give this up and in the spirit of transparency, masturbation as well. However, God was calling me to engage in a lifestyle of celibacy.

I remember the day I made that decision, I was in a relationship with a man that I decided to date. We were as physical as physical could get, but as I started to change, my desire for sex started to change. When I told the guy how I felt he dropped me like a bad habit. In all honesty I couldn't even be mad, God was doing something, and I had to be ok with the results. Even if that meant losing what I thought would last.

So, for those of you who think that you must be perfect before you get serious with God, let me tell you, THAT is not the case. Some Christians may use the term "come as you are" which means that the body of believers should be accepting of you regardless of what state you are in.

That statement doesn't reference wearing a certain type of clothing or looking a certain way. It means, no matter what you have on, how you look or what condition you're in, God welcomes you without judgement and will forgive your sins. Nevertheless, some believers tend to use that phrase out of context. I personally, think it means to bring all your issues, the things you struggle with, and the matters of your heart to Him and He will give you rest.

> **(Matthew 11:28 KJV)** *"Come unto me, all ye that labour and are heavy laden, and I will give you rest."*

So, get in God's face, pray for understanding and He will reveal what is right and wrong. Those habits you wish to get rid of, allow Him to expose the truth about it and He will take the desires away from you.

Time to Reflect: *So, let's be truthful my Love, what are some bad habits you possess? Do you think you need to give them up? Do they aid in your benefit to grow? What are some things that you are holding on to? Why are you holding on? Are there some people in your life that you need to let go? Who would you identify as your core circle and will they pray for you and strengthen you in your time of need? If you don't possess a core, who do you have in mind to link up with?*

Chapter Seven
Don't Push Me, I'm close To the Edge

When someone says they are close to the edge, you can only picture them on the edge of a huge cliff. They are about to jump into complete and utter destruction. Can you imagine how we can reach that point mentally? As a fully functional adult, I never thought I would face that close to the edge experience, anxiety is real.

Dealing with anxiety was one of the few times in my life where I didn't have full control over my mind and body. When I wanted to sleep, I couldn't, when I wanted to rest, I couldn't. Imagine being on edge 24/7, constantly putting your body through overdrive and your heart beating at alarming rates. Experiencing breathless moments, sweating and hyperventilating, ending up in a hospital with the thought of a possible heart attack.

I found myself sitting on the edge of an examining table, talking to a nurse and balling my eyes out. I guess in her mind I was battling depression, but I just wanted to sleep at that moment. It had been three days and I was functioning on four hours of sleep. I worried myself so much that I put my body through extreme stress. The sad part is that I had no warning sign, no heads up, I was mentally on a cliff with a push that I didn't see coming.

Anxiety is simply excessive and persistent worrying and fear in simple situations. To be honest with you, writing about this brings me back to that place. I just know I didn't like what I did to myself.

I later went to my doctor's office to search for solutions. They gave me a questionnaire that asked me, once again if I was depressed, OMG…NO I'M NOT DEPRESSED. If someone asks me this one more time, I'm going to lose it. Clearly, I was ignorant to the matter, as depression and anxiety go hand in hand. I didn't care what I was, I just wanted to sleep. What I didn't understand was that there is a direct correlation between the body, mind, and spirit.

The issues that I had going on in my mind, affected what was going on in my body and did a number on my spirit. Once again, I'm balling my eyes out on the examining table. So, after talking to me and listening to what I felt, they concluded that they would prescribe drugs.

What's crazy is that the doctor suggested that I talk to a therapist. It was then when I connected the dots. I went in to check my physical, but I still had to work on my mental and spiritual. The physical dysfunction was only a manifestation of what had been going on inside of me, so I had to deal with all aspects of myself. Thank God I had a life coach, Godly praying parents and a few Godly friends assigned to my life, so I was able to call for help.

Here is a side note, let's be clear, I used to be a person who didn't really accept help. I felt I could do things on my own, I was too proud to look vulnerable, because receiving help made me feel like I was weak and incapable. Maybe it had something to do with other people's perception of me because my image is what I always held onto.

I was so busy looking and being the part on a constant basis, not realizing that I put enormous demands on myself by being everything for everybody. By this time, I was over it all, I needed help and I needed it fast. I had to put my pride aside because I was sinking fast, thank you Jesus for my life lines.

I had to make some serious decisions when I left the doctor's office. Do I rely on this medication to dictate my feelings, body and my spirit? Or, do I deal with the real issues at hand? Relying on medication seemed so forced and totally outside of my nature. I didn't want to have to depend on a substance to control me, so I prayed and decided to let God take control, His therapy was all I needed.

I had a real conversation with my Heavenly Father, and I said "this is not how I plan to stay. I don't see this as a way of life. Dad, you have got to take me through this.

"My days will get better, and I will trust that you will order my steps, no matter how anxious it makes me feel." From that moment on I was determined to walk through the root issues that caused my body to go in to overdrive.

Looking back at that moment, I realized that God requires us to have faith. However, in that faith we are required to move. You see, God already has your path laid out, but your faith is executed when you walk it. Faith without works is dead.

> **(James 2:17 KJV) "Even so faith, if it has not works, is dead being alone."**

Subconsciously, I used the power of faith in that moment. I just knew I didn't want to spend my days on medication, so it was that same drive that made me activate the faith that I'd been resting on.

There is no magic as to how I overcame this circumstance. As a matter of fact, I still have moments when I start to freak out when I can't see God's movement. But He consistently reminds me of how I overcame that situation. If I'm strong enough to endure that, I'm strong enough to endure everything else. I had to learn to trust God no matter what the process looked like.

Dealing with root issues is something we need to be prepared to do. It's easy to lie to yourself and say that you are fine and that you will get past it. It's like sweeping dust under the rug every day. Over time you can't ignore the hump that's mounting underneath it. Dust can seem so small, but if you collect enough of it, it becomes extremely visible.

A lot of us make the mistake of living life and dealing with what comes with it. Nevertheless, all the things that we learn along the way determines how we deal with the rest of it. Some results are good, some are bad, some results are negative, and some are positive.

Time to Reflect: *So, let's begin to connect your dots. Are you anxious about anything? Are there moments when you slide into depression? What has happened in your life to trigger moments of depression and\or anxiety for you? Do you feel it's something that you can control? What issues lie underneath your rug? Have you carefully evaluated those issues to come up with some solutions?*

I ended up becoming spiritually connected to a woman who worked with me and she began to reveal a dream to me. In her dream, she saw me in a lake or some sort of body of water, and I was barely staying afloat. My response to her was HOW DID YOU KNOW? Because that's exactly how I felt.

All the changes that I had made were nice and I've learned so much from them. I have received so much revelation, gotten so close to God and became spiritually in tuned with him. I was so in tuned that for every worry I had, God would instantly address my concerns however, I was becoming a little impatient. Okay, more like a lot impatient because I felt like I had sacrificed so much.

I was doing everything that I was told to do, I became better at controlling my behavior and I had stopped worrying. I stayed constantly in God's presence by reading scripture and meditating on his word. I was going to church on Sundays as well as attending weekly bible study, but I was still wondering WHEN?

When were things going to break for me? I was peeling back layers and becoming more and more exposed. I was no longer the person that I started out as in this journey, I was morphing into something else.

As humans, we are so complexed, the idea of transformation is a beautiful thing, but we are made up of flesh, emotions, and certain intricacies. We have to fight through so much of ourselves in order to change and it takes a strong disciplined mind to be adamant about those changes. I would like to believe that's why God allowed me to discipline myself from my old habits.

When I think of a caterpillar, its sole purpose is to become a butterfly. The first stage of its metamorphosis is the Egg which symbolized the beginning of my journey. The second stage is the Larva where it is feed, this symbolized my period of being nurtured for growth.

The third stage is the Pupa also known as the cocoon which symbolized my quiet period, being isolated, developed and protected for my transformation. Finally stage four, the Adult phase where I was ready to reveal my evolution into something that is fearfully and wonderfully made by God. You see, this change had to take place on the inside so that God's glory could be revealed on the outside.

> (***Psalms 139:14 KJV***) *"I will praise thee, for I am fearfully and wonderfully made: marvelous are thy works; and that my soul knoweth right well."*

I'm not claiming to be strong by any means and I will be the first to tell you that I have no clue as to how I was able to accomplish this. All I knew was that my relationship with God had changed to the point where I was as brutally honest with Him as I could possibly be.

I expressed every emotion that I felt, no matter how much I wanted to hide from Him, I had to be real. He honored my relationship with Him. He became more than what I could ever imagine Him to me. He was a combination of father, best friend, leader and counselor.

We think we can hide from God but we just have to be realistic with ourselves. If He knows everything about us, then why not share our feelings and struggles. It was in confessing my faults to Him that he began to deal with me personally.

He gave me strength during times when I was falling apart. I can't tell you how many times I spent my nights in tears and crying myself to sleep, praying that He would just see me through. I was a very vocal about what I was feeling because I needed God to audibly hear my voice so that I could be confident that He was listening.

I was told by someone special in my life that the biggest cliché of the African American woman is that we have to be strong. When in fact, it's that 'have to be' part that destroys us because it puts us in a place of being viewed as a super woman.

Who says we have to be strong, putting up a front like we have it all together when we are really falling apart on the inside. We are afraid to be vulnerable because if we show that we are hurting it is a sign of weakness. That itself is a lot to live up to and further adds to the pressures of life.

God tells us in His word to confess our faults one to another that we might be delivered. Your healing comes from sharing your struggles with others so that they may benefit from hearing your testimony.

> *(James 5:16a KJV) "Confess your faults one to another, and pray one for another, that ye may be healed."*

Don't get me wrong, everyone is not for you, so you must be careful about who you confess your faults to or open up to. Remember, I had that select few who walked with me in my season of transformation. They were the ones that God and I trusted.

Even Jesus had a select few, although He was surrounded by His twelve disciples, there was only three, who were considered as His best friends and inner circle. Because He trusted them, they were privileged to see His transfiguration and witness Him in all of His glory.

God will surround you with a few trustworthy people in your life who will be there when you are going through your struggles. These people are there to witness your growth and celebrate your glory.

Time to Reflect: Let's think! If you could be completely honest, what is God doing in your life that you are not too happy with? Have you expressed that to Him? What do you need to do in order to make a transformation?

Chapter Eight
I see the Light

For the first time in my life, I was being completely honest with myself. Accepting all truths and owning my feelings, I became open with my Heavenly Father. Understanding that He is in love with me and He longs for the moments of us spending time together.

Because of His loving kindness, which drew me closer to him, we became something that I hadn't had in a very long time, we became intimate.

> *(Jeremiah 31:3 KJV) "The Lord hath appeared of old unto me, saying, yea, I have loved thee with an everlasting love: therefore with loving kindness have I drawn thee."*

What's strange is how being intimate with God allowed me to strengthen my relationships with others. I had lost sight of the things around me, having tunnel vision and only being focus on what I was doing and nothing else. Truth be told, there were no ill intentions, I was just absorbed in what I was doing and what I wanted so much so that I allowed it to consume me.

However, as I began to get closer with God, I started to appreciate life's precious moments. I learned to slow down in this rat race of life, and I learned to live my best life. I had to stop and smell the roses and be thankful for the things that God had blessed me with. Somehow, I had lost sight of what it feels like to actually live and not worry about anything, I had finally found my peace.

> ***(Philippians 4:6, 7 KJV) "Be careful for nothing, but in everything by prayer and supplication with thanksgiving let your requests be made known unto God. And the peace of God which passeth all understanding, shall keep your hearts and minds through Christ Jesus."***

One of the hardest parts of my journey was taking it one day at a time. Sounds crazy right? Well it's definitely something I was not use to. I am the type of person that was enthralled in my work. Trying to climb the corporate ladder and feeling unaccomplished if I was stagnated in my current position.

I wanted to accomplish so much, but I felt like time wasn't on my side. I was in a hurry to get things done. I would often think about my future, worrying about how I was going to get things done. To be honest that was an exhausting way to live. I would get anxiety on just wondering if I was going to get married, or have children, because in my mind, being in your thirties with no husband and children by society's standard was unimaginable.

Oh....and the questions that I get asked when I meet new people. Are you married? Do you have any children? How old are you? Sometimes it's enough to make you want to scream. Or, when I look on social media and I see someone that I know flashing a pretty diamond ring on their finger, saying "I said yes". It is enough to make you insane, yet it is in those moments that I look up at God and say "Ok God, I'm waiting"

I'm pretty sure He laughs at my impatience, but He shows me that everything you see is not what it appears to be. He, then allows me to see those couples who are having major issues because they didn't discover themselves before they got married.

So now they must deal with not only themselves, but their spouses who also didn't take the time to discover themselves before marriage. Or the insecure women that I see on social media who needs the approval of society to feel validated. "Ok God....I get it".

He is constantly reminding me why my relationship with Him is important and why His timing is everything. I can remember waking up one morning and feeling like the world had been lifted off my shoulders.

After spending so much time changing and feeling like I was being broken, God had to show me the light and it was suddenly. There is a time and season for everything under the sun and He has made everything beautiful in His time.

> *(Eccl 3:11 KJV) "He hath made everything beautiful in his time: also he hath set the world in their hearts, so that no man can find out that God maketh from the beginning to the end."*

I needed my time of deconstruction, it was then that God could reconstruct me from the beginning to the end. I had to feel that pain and be able walk through it so that I could discover the source of my issues. The greatest thing about this was God never let me do this thing by myself. He gave me my inner circle, the support of my family, and He Himself held me through many nights.

I was going through a detox and he was cleansing me. When alcoholics or drug addicts stop using substances, their bodies go through periods of withdrawal. Sometimes the symptoms of withdrawal can be volatile and very unbearable, yet this cleansing is essential for their recovery.

I remember feeling anxious because I didn't want to be celibate anymore and longing for intimacy. I wanted to be held, cuddled and caressed, but I had to hold my pillow instead and just pray that God would see me through. I now, know that this period of withdrawal was necessary for my spiritual growth.

God is a God of discipline and order, He is also a God of compassion. So, when I pleaded to Him about having someone in my life, He began to remind me that not everyone is worthy of my time and space. I couldn't afford to entertain anyone who was not wise enough and who wasn't governed by Him. He further reminded me that I couldn't let anyone interfere with what He was reconstructing.

He had been trying to let me see all along that I was worth it. To love Him first, then myself, and then love others. That's why my foundation and my faith was so important. Whenever things just didn't feel right to me, I would instantly go into praise and worship.

That was truly the only thing that allowed me to survive this process. In my praise and worship I got so close to Him and my moments of agony became moments of gratitude and appreciation. It is when you are in the midst of trials and tribulation that you fight with praise. I learned to combat the devil because if I didn't give Him any ammunition to penetrate my mind, He couldn't torment me.

God inhabits the praises of His people and it is our praise that shifts the atmosphere. I noticed that when I gave all my worries to Him and learned to praise and worship Him that I began to feel better. And it's not something that comes naturally, I had to be able to discipline myself and make it an automatic response.

Time to Reflect: *At what moment do you feel God lifting burdens off your shoulders? What practices help you to discipline yourself and your mindset? If no practices are identified, what are some ways you can began to train your mindset? What trigger moments do you experience that takes you off focus? What robs you of the peace that you deserve? What are some ways you can fight for your peace?*

Chapter Nine
Faith without Works

Faith without works is.... I'm pretty sure you know the rest. Faith is often talked about in church and it is one of the cornerstones of Christianity. Being able to believe in the very thing that you can't see. In order to please God, it is a must that you have faith. However, God has given every man a measure of faith, so it's important that you build upon that faith.

> *(Romans 12:3 KJV) "For I say, through the grace give unto me, to every man that is among you, not to think of himself more highly than he ought to think; but to think soberly, according as God hath dealth to every man the measure of faith."*

What's interesting is that you don't even have to have much faith. It is said that having faith the size of mustard seed is all that is required. Why is it that the mustard seed is compared to the measure of faith needed? If you think about, the mustard seed is indeed the smallest of all seeds on earth but once planted and cultivated it can produce huge branches.

Now, it is quite obvious that this comparison is made because of the simple fact that faith, like the mustard seed, can be cultivated. Faith has the potential of being full grown and stronger than anything. But there is one thing that we forget, without putting the work in it doesn't grow. So yes, faith is very important in your spiritual walk and yes, you must do the work.

I can recall asking God to increase my measure of faith. Boy, why did I ask that? You should always be careful what you ask for, you just might get it. It's when I asked for it that He went to work. I started to be faced with so much opposition until I couldn't see clearly.

I began to question God as to why I must go through this, He quickly reminded me of my request. I had to humble myself because my initial reaction was to act out of character. After He reminded me of what His purpose was for me, I had to bite the bullet and learn how to work through these tests with grace.

Have you ever been under attack and had to go through it with grace? Something that we very seldom do because our flesh reacts to the circumstances that surround us. Nevertheless, when God works Faith in us, He reminds us to trust Him. Not only that but He sends all kinds of messages, signs, words, people, and so much more to confirm what He is doing.

That's one of the things that I love about God. When I went through my tests and trials, He gave me so many resources to rely upon that helped me to get through it. He spoke to me through so many things, and that alone allowed me to understand that I was comforted, protected, loved, and most of all on the right course.

With His help and resources, I tapped into cultivating my faith, so what started as a mustard seed ended up sprouting into something bigger. However, it took work, you see, you must be able to do your work. This journey of building character is not something that you can just sit back and receive. Nor is it something that is readily given when you ask for it. It takes sacrifice, releasing the things that you hold on to, and letting go of the people you love, basically changing from the inside out. Old habits had to go, and I had a FIT, don't get me wrong, I love change, but I don't love the process of changing.

I found out that the idea of faith is to be able to release into the atmosphere what you want and commit yourself to Him and He will give you the desires of your heart.

> *(Psalms 37:4 KJV) "Delight thyself also in the Lord: and he shall give thee the desires of thine heart."*

It's possible that God will honor your wishes, but you must understand His timing, this is where faith comes in. You must have faith to know that God will give you the desires of your heart, and that means trusting in Him for your every need and He will satisfy your earthy desires.

For an example, by the end of 2014 I was interested in buying a fur coat. At the time I was living in Chicago, so a fur coat was a necessity for the brutally cold temperatures there. Any who, I told God that I thought it would be cool to have it, so I prayed about it and I left it alone.

Around October of that same year I decided to go and look for the fur coat. So, I along with my mom, who is my biggest supporter and the owner of several furs, I went to a furrier near my home.

There were so many different styles of furs to choose from so I was immediately overwhelmed. I picked up one coat that cost $8,000 and then another one that cost $10,000 and another one for $9,500. These were the prices of cars and down payments to houses, and I couldn't afford any of them.

My mom suggested that I choose one, try it on and if I liked it to finance it. However, I knew that I wouldn't be able to afford the monthly payments, but when I put the coat on, I instantly felt like it was mine. It looked so good and it was exactly what I had envisioned, a short asymmetric black mink jacket, I fell in love.

I modeled in it and walked back and forth, I was truly feeling myself until I looked at the price tag. I instantly dropped my head, I was so defeated, I just couldn't afford it, so I took it off and hung it back up. Before I walked out of the door, the sales person asked for my email address so that I could be added to their email list. I had to admit I was slightly disappointed, but I reluctantly gave it to her and went on with my life.

By March 2015, I received an email from the same furrier letting me know that they were having a major sale. I grabbed my mom again and said let's give it another try, so we went back to the furrier. When we arrived, we began to look again to see what they had, as we were looking at all the coats, my mom spotted the same coat that I had tried on during our last visit. It was in the same spot and looked like it had never been moved, so I tried it on again and it again felt just like home, LOL.

I remember not being able to afford it the last time, so I immediately looked at the price. I didn't realize that the purpose of the sale was to liquidate last year's inventory and the reduction was 60 to 80 % off the lowest ticketed price. I asked the sales person how much the cost would be. The coat went from $8,000 to $6,000 with an additional 80% off that price.

After she calculated the final price, it was a little over a thousand dollars. She then structured the terms of the payment plan over a year which made it very affordable and all I had to do was make a small down payment. I couldn't believe what I was hearing, that coat could actually be mine. I faithfully paid the payments on time and by New Year's Eve, when it was 16 degrees outside, I was strutting into watch night service in my brand new black mink jacket, Hallelujah!!!

I said all that to say this, God knows the desires of your heart. The process of getting that coat revealed quite a few things about Him to me. I didn't get it when I asked for it because I had to be patient and wait. I learned that the process of waiting was to make obtaining the coat a whole lot easier on my pockets and my budget.

It showed me that when I told Him what I wanted, He didn't ignore me. He had every intention of giving me what I asked for, He just had to create the right circumstance for me to get it so that I wouldn't have any struggles paying for it.

> **(Proverbs 10:22 KJV) "The blessings of the Lord, it maketh rich, and he addeth no sorrow to it."**

I can remember a time where I was extremely impatient with God. I wanted things done when I wanted it and became so furious when I didn't get my way. I know, I sound like a brat, don't I? But in exuding that type of behavior, I messed up a lot of blessings for myself.

Not understanding that God is strategic and organized in everything that He does. I showed Him that He couldn't trust me, so I had to suffer many times because of my actions. I was responsible in orchestrating my own downfall, making Him out to be something that He was trying to prove to me repeatedly that He wasn't. Boy, was I immature, but in the process, I've learned patience, which is the hardest fruit to master. I had put God in a box with my own thinking and expected Him to perform according to what I wanted Him to do. How selfish was I, which was another pill I had to swallow.

We say that God is the ruler of everything, but do we treat Him like that? Instead we treat Him like a genie, expecting for our wishes to be granted on command. What's crazy is that sometimes He does, because He is such a gracious God but when that behavior gets in the way of spiritual maturity, He then must take parental actions.

Think about it. Do you give your kids EVERYTHING they want? If you did, you would spoil them rotten. You must make children work for what they want. My mom taught me the value of work when I was young. It started with assigning me weekly chores when I was about the age of seven. Once my chores were done, I was given an allowance and rewarded for my good work. As I grew older it taught me the importance of hard work. My parents made me understand that if I ever wanted something in this world, I had to work for it.

Though, I didn't have to work for everything, some things were given to me as well. However, there was a healthy balance, I never really expected for everything to just be given to me. So, as I grew older, I developed a great work ethic. I also developed a love for the finer things, but I knew I had to work for them.

Much like myself, I'm sure you have many things before the Lord, praying that He would manifest them. We know He is able to give us the desires of our heart and we know that He can give things to us beyond our wildest expectations, but He requires us to move. It is said that without Faith it is impossible to please God.

> *(Hebrews 11:6 KJV) "But without faith it is impossible to please him, for he that cometh to God must believe that he is, and that he is a rewarder of them that diligently seek him."*

Again, our faith is connected to trusting God, so when our faith lacks, our trust in God lacks as well. Do you think that is a functional relationship? Think about it like this, if you've been in a relationship you know that it takes communication, commitment and trust. When you connect to someone who you don't trust, it changes the dynamics of the relationship. After a while the relationship fades away and then becomes nonexistent.

Time to Reflect: *Assess the measure of faith you have. Is your faith enough to sustain you? What areas in your life do you struggle to have faith in? Are you willing to go through in order to grow you portion of faith?*

How Tedious was your journey?

Let's be truthful. our journey never ends. Life continues to teach us the lessons that we need to learn. Every situation is an introspective moment and a reflection on yourself, never take for granted the lessons that life teaches. It's only when you change your perspective that you open yourself up to learn the lesson.

It took me a long time to write this book, and I had my reservation on whether to finish it. I was simply afraid of this project not being effective. After much prayer and meditation, God made me realize that this is bigger than me. That someone out there has a similar journey and had some serious questions.

You see, my journey continues, I never stop learning, nor do I stop growing. In fact, I still have my moments when I need to look inside myself. This process isn't an overnight adventure, it took a few years for me to get a grip. However, I continue to face many situations that challenge my spiritualty, growth and wisdom.

To those of you who continue to get hit by life, and you have no idea of the outcome or how things will turn out, I encourage you to keep fighting. There is a purpose for your pain. I've spent nights in tears, not understanding why God was digging so deep in my foundation. There were days where I was barely making it. Praying that one day I would stop walking this tedious journey. Every day was a fight and a struggle to just get out of bed, let alone go through the day.

I'll tell you what's important, connect with a support system that will encourage you. Pray that God surrounds you with people who hear from God, that know how to get a prayer though and who can give you sound spiritual advice. The will to want to be better takes yourself, but the endurance of the journey takes a team. Be all you can be in this lifetime. Make this current life your best life and remember sharing is important as well. Your testimony is someone else's current journey and your words could help inspire them. I want to end with this a prayer.

Father in Heaven, You're an awesome God. The ultimate dad in our lives. I pray for the lovely soul holding this book. I pray that something was said to inspire your dear child. We are all your children, trying so desperately to figure this life out. And no, we don't have all the answers but every day I pray that you reveal to us truth, wisdom, and love. We understand that it is not of our own strength that we make it, but by your grace, mercy, and power.

Continue to love us though this journey. For there is much to learn and knowledge to gain. Help us to be better people for those close to us. Allow us to be the light that draws man to you. Help us to understand our purpose and to live that very purpose here on earth. We can't do this without you. So, we ask for clarity and direction for our lives.

We know life will continue to hit us, but I pray that you hold our hands through it all. And when we are not sure that you are there, give us a constant reminder that you stand with us. Give us strength when we are weak. Give us the tools to withstand the enemy. And we will praise your name forever more, In Jesus Holy Name, Amen

Until next time I'm Nastassia and this is my tedious journey.

Prayer List

Answered Prayers

www.ingramcontent.com/pod-product-compliance
Lightning Source LLC
LaVergne TN
LVHW051843080426
835512LV00018B/3041